BROKEN TOY
HERO

BY JOHN BUCKLAND

Broken Toy Hero

Published by:
HAVAH Publishing
Ashland, OH
amy@havahpublishing.com
www.havahpublishing.com

Address all inquiries to:
John Buckland
h4hcharity@yahoo.com
H4HCharity.org
www.BTWV.us

ISBN: 978-1-64751-020-6
Library of Congress Control Number: 2019956453

Editor and Interior Book Layout: Amy Rice
Cover Designer: Geremy Woods, CEO of Timeless Acrylics

Printed in the United States of America

Second Edition

Dedication:

*First, I want to thank God for everything in my life-the good and the bad. It was the tough things in my life that worked within me to help forge me into who I am today.
*Thank you to my amazing family. You have all been so supportive and patient as you watch me pursue dream after dream for my life. I love living the dream together!
*Thank you to all the amazing people who have supported and believed in me the entire way. Always remember when you look at my life: All of you can take credit for giving me a piece of your goodness to help make me who I am today. *A very special thank you to Phyllis and Vernon Bell of Scott Sullivan Incorporated for sponsoring all the artwork for this first book. You are the most supportive in-laws a person could have. I truly appreciate you both. *Thank you to everyone who reads this book and shares what they learn with the rest of the world. Together, we can inspire others to be overcomers as well!

Every so often long-awaited toys showed up at the store. Phoenix was a special toy. She was beautiful and popular, and the day came when she was on the shelf. *I will end up with a special child, one to love me and hold me. My child will take me everywhere they go,* Phoenix happily thought.

Phoenix sat in her box waiting for her child and imagined all the things they would do together. *We will practice flying through the yard, my child holding me. I will sit by my boy or girl while they eat. They will love me and tell everyone that I am their favorite toy. We will grow together, go places and see things. At night, they will take me in the bath to make me squeaky clean. Then we will get tucked in snug and tight for sleep.*

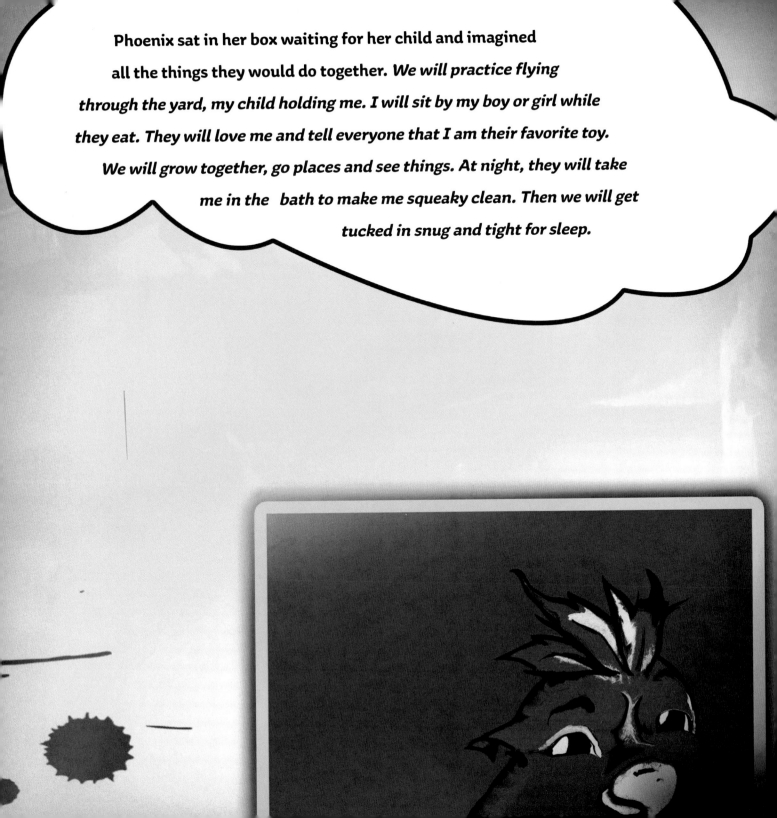

Dreaming was easy and good in the box. Finally, the day came when the daydreams were interrupted by a child: Phoenix's child.

Phoenix focused her eyes on a boy who had brown hair and bright blue eyes. She imagined that he was as kind as he looked, when she heard him say, "Mom! This is Phoenix. Mom, look how cool!!! I need her, please buy her for me!"

Mom answered, "She is special, did you see all the things she can say? Of course, you can get her!"

Phoenix felt herself being lifted from the shelf. She knew that she had found her child.

On the car ride home, the little boy talked to Phoenix, "My name is Adam, and you are my favorite toy ever. I like that you are shiny and strong. You will be my bestest friend!" Phoenix loved everything that Adam was saying, *I am so happy that this is my new family,* she thought. They pulled up in front of a white house. Adam ran towards the green door with Phoenix in his hand.

"Come meet everybody. Dad, this is Phoenix. Mom, Phoenix. Phoenix this is my cat, Lily, and my sister, Jen."

Phoenix looked around and saw other toys on the floor, scattered all around. *Surely, Adam will never leave me on the floor,* she thought. Adam decided to play with Phoenix. He threw her into the air. Phoenix enjoyed the flight until she crashed into the ground, chipping paint from her beautiful tail. *Ouch!* *It was an accident that he didn't catch me.*

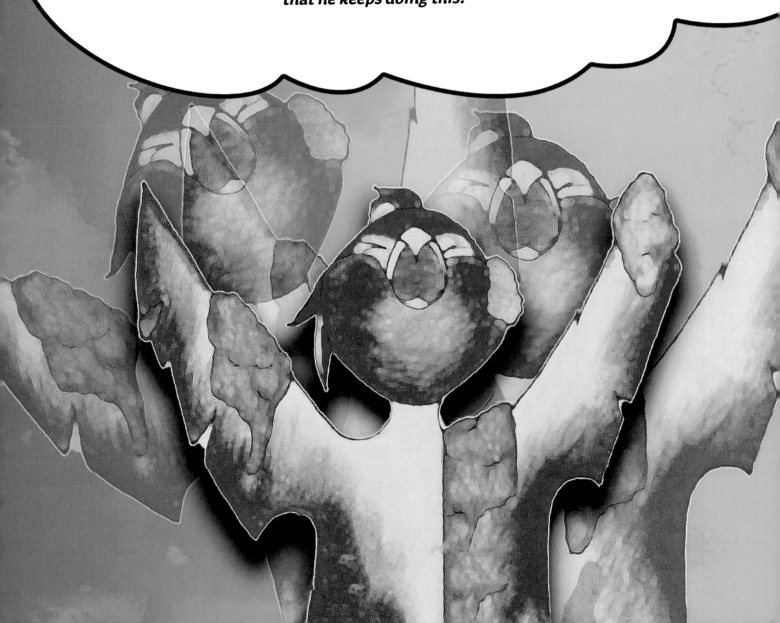

Adam picked Phoenix up and ran outside into the yard with her. She liked the sunshine and was ready to conquer Adam's imaginary worlds. She was shocked when Adam dropkicked her, and she landed in a muddy puddle. *NO!* she screamed inwardly, *this is not how I was meant to be played with. It isn't right that he keeps doing this!*

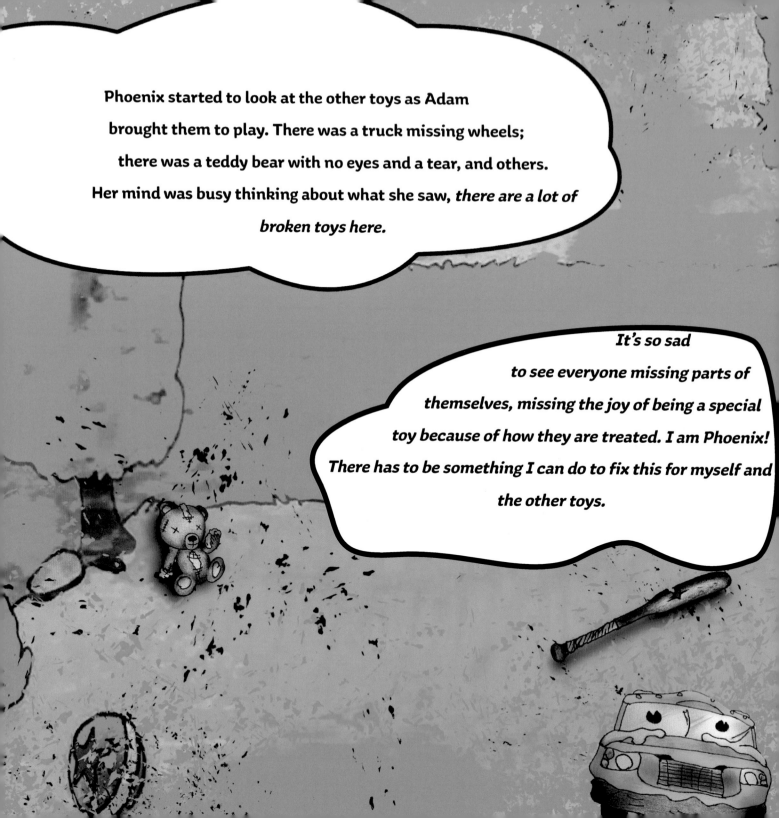

Phoenix started to look at the other toys as Adam brought them to play. There was a truck missing wheels; there was a teddy bear with no eyes and a tear, and others. Her mind was busy thinking about what she saw, *there are a lot of broken toys here.*

It's so sad to see everyone missing parts of themselves, missing the joy of being a special toy because of how they are treated. I am Phoenix! There has to be something I can do to fix this for myself and the other toys.

The days continued and Adam kept mistreating Phoenix. She was crushed by the heartbreak she felt. She had wanted to be loved by her child, and she had imagined a completely different life. When the night started to wind down, Phoenix waited to be taken to bed to rest with Adam and found that she was thrown by the wayside.

"Adam, clean up your toys before you go to bed," Mom called.

Phoenix waited and waited to be picked up by Adam. Realization set in that he wasn't coming. She felt toy tears moisten her cheeks.

The house grew quiet, and Phoenix felt herself being lifted, "All these dumb toys left out. I am tired of picking them all up every day," Mom complained as she threw Phoenix into the toybox.

As Phoenix crashed into the other toys, she saw the stars from a cosmic light projector illuminate the ceiling of the toybox. She isn't sure when she drifted to sleep, but the stars were the last thing she saw.

Phoenix dreamed of the times that she had been treated unfairly. The times that Adam had stuffed her down the drain in the bathtub. She thought about the paint that changed her colors from radiant to dingy. She cringed at the thought of him stomping on her and ripping out her pull string. She cried in her sleep thinking of how he told her he didn't love her anymore and she wasn't his favorite toy.

As Phoenix slept, a dream came, and a shiny gorgeous toy spoke to her: "No matter how broken you are and no matter how hard life is, you can change, and you can do good. It is never too late to help other broken toys learn they can be good too. In order for you to learn how to do this, there are four things for you to learn, Phoenix. If you do these four things every day, you can be as great as you want to be in your life and you can be the toy that everybody wants to play with. You can be the toy everybody looks up to."

When Phoenix woke up, she looked around. The toys that had been shadows the night before had faces. She looked at them in their states of brokenness. Her dream began to come back to her. She pushed the button on the cosmic light projector to see that it didn't work. *Maybe I am imagining the dream,* she pondered. *There is only one way to know for sure.* Phoenix decided to try the four steps that the shiny toy had taught her in her dream.

Phoenix planned to teach the other toys what she had learned. She knew the best way was to be an example. She grabbed the worn-out hammerhead shark puppet who was missing his eyes, and told him, "Of the things we have to remember every day: Number 1. Never give up. You must realize, Hammer, that life is not always going to be easy. Life is not always going to be fair. Always remember the tough things in life are things that make great people, and you will be great too." Phoenix noticed how easily she repeated every word she had been told by the shiny toy. This excited her as she continued on to the next toy.

Hammer's eyes lit up from where they were missing. He transformed right in front of the othe[r] toys. His fur became soft and full again. The tear where a hand belonged went back togethe[r], only leaving a small stitch in a different color to show that he had ever been torn. Hamme[r] the Hammerhead smiled and said, "Phoenix, I will never give up! You have given me hope! My future will be to inspire other toys and children to be kind and keep going n[o] matter what may happen to them! Thank you for your help."

Hero Girl felt her hair growing back and smiled as she realized her new hair was growing in a brilliant gold.

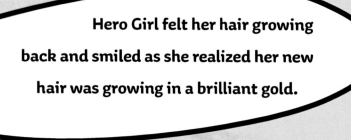

"Phoenix, I will do the right thing no matter how anyone treats me. I forgot that somehow, but now that you reminded me, I am happy to show others the right things to do. I will start by saying kind things to all the other toys. It's been a long time since we heard anything nice."
Hero Girl felt the change and the peace that came with the decision to go back to doing the right things.

"3. Help other people. There are many toys around you that are broken. The only way that they can see a way out is if another toy rises and becomes everything that they deserve to be. The best way to do this is to make a choice that you are going to take the tough things in your life and put them to work for the good of other people. You will be the toy that other toys look up to and find hope in."

Smaller toys were coming forward to watch the magic of kindness continue to unfold. It was contagious.

Phoenix continued, "The more good things that you do for other toys, the more great things will happen in your life. Every time you do something good for somebody else your scars will heal. Every time you do good for somebody else you will become better and stronger than ever." Phoenix was building in excitement as the toys cheered.

Bobby revved his engine. Everyone looked at him and gasped. His missing wheels had grown back in a brilliant gold.

Bobby started to speak in excitement, "I will help other people as often as I can! Look at my wheels! Helping others makes us better for sure. Phoenix helped me and my wheels are here and better than ever! Thank you Phoenix, we can never stop helping others."

"There is only one more piece to this puzzle. Penny the Parasaurolophus where are you? Can you come here?" Phoenix paused as she waited to hear Penny answer.
"Has anyone seen Penny?" Phoenix quizzed the toys.
There was a whisper as Penny poked her head through a doll blanket, "I am right here. Please don't let anyone make fun of me anymore...I'd rather be thrown away than keep hearing how funny I look, and how I'm not as cool as a T-rex or triceratops."

"Oh, Penny, I would NEVER say those awful things to you. You are perfect for the final thing that we all need to remember every day," Phoenix began.

"I am? Oh, please tell us!" Penny excitedly interrupted.

She was starting to stand taller because Phoenix had chosen her. This was the first time in a long time that she had been chosen for anything at all, and her confidence was building.

"4. Never be a bully. You must always remember: No matter how tough life has been as a toy and no matter how bad your family has been to you, never use that as an excuse to mistreat other people. Treat other people with respect and kindness because you never know what other toys are going through. Every toy has some sort of scar, but some toys have more scars than others and not everybody can see those scars. Some of those scars go really deep. So, Penny, you must be the toy that treats other toys with total respect and teaches them to do the same. It is in treating others with dignity, kindness, and respect that you will become the toy hero," Phoenix finished the four steps.

Penny's smile disappeared. "It is hard to be nice when it seems that everyone is so mean to me. Is it still bullying to be mean to the toys that make fun of me? Do I have to be nice to even them to be a toy hero?"

Phoenix cupped her jaw in her hand, "Yes, you should be kind even to those who are mean to you. It is harder to do that, but your kindness could change them too! Then they might be nice to others because you showed them how. That's a big deal, huh, Penny?"

"Golly, it sounds hard, but from the way you explain it...it will be worth it! I will be nice even to the toys that are mean to me, Phoenix."

As Penny changed from the inside out, she grew a few inches, and her colors became dazzling. The chips in her paint were filled in with gold.

The crowd of toys was starting to talk all at once. Phoenix yelled, "Quiet, let me finish please!" The toybox grew quiet. She continued, "You will become the Toy Hero that other toys will want to be like. Your life has been tough, but it has been tough for a reason. Now, you must realize that the whole reason behind your tough life is so that you can teach others and show other toys how to overcome. Regardless of what you see when you look at yourself, you are all capable of becoming toy heroes. You are the broken toy heroes that the world needs to see. Do these four things every day and you can be as great as you want to be."

As Phoenix finished, she
realized that she had repeated every word
that the shiny toy had taught her. A blinding light filled the toybox,
and all the toys shielded their eyes from the dazzling colors that were
flying around. Nothing like this had ever happened in a toybox anywhere. They
were speechless with amazement.

When the light cleared, Phoenix stood for all the toys to see, transformed by the message she had been given in a dream and shared. You could still see her broken places, they had become a permanent part of her, yet they were somehow beautiful as she had helped to share the transforming message. Everyone wanted to be like Phoenix, so the toys set out to help and heal each other, teaching toys that hadn't heard the message so that they could be fixed too.

Adam brought friends over that fateful day. He opened the toybox, saw all of the toys fixed, and slammed the lid down, breathing hard. How had this happened? Surely, his parents hadn't stayed up to fix his toys...

He picked up Phoenix first and pulled her string.

"Never give up," she chirped. She hadn't said that before, so he pulled the string again, "Always do the right thing."

His mouth hung open as he kept pulling the string that had been missing, "Help other people. Never be a bully."

This time, Adam didn't throw her to the ground. His friends started to marvel over her, she was nothing like their Phoenix toys. She was special.

Phoenix heard their kind words and decided to share a message with even them, and with you reading this now:

"Inside of each of us, inside of every person, inside of every boy and every girl is a broken toy hero. A broken toy hero that the world is waiting on to rise."

Now, it's your turn to practice the 4 Steps to Greatness:

1. Never give _____.
2. Always do the _____ thing.
3. _____ other people.
4. Never be a _____.

Together, we can make the world a better place.
Every person that makes positive changes and treats others

with kindness makes a difference.
You may not see it right away or in everybody,
but it is still the best thing to do!

You are a hero too!

Go to WWW.BTWV.US

Select the "After Story Discussion" Button.

Made in the USA
Columbia, SC
23 April 2022

59285505R00024